THIS BOOK BELONGS TO:

Made in the USA
Monee, IL
01 July 2022

98936603R00072